AF270207

Gross Jokes

Joe King

Abdo Kids Junior
is an Imprint of Abdo Kids
abdobooks.com

Abdo
ABDO KIDS JOKES
Kids

abdobooks.com

Published by Abdo Kids, a division of ABDO, P.O. Box 398166, Minneapolis, Minnesota 55439.
Copyright © 2022 by Abdo Consulting Group, Inc. International copyrights reserved in all countries.
No part of this book may be reproduced in any form without written permission from the publisher.
Abdo Kids Junior™ is a trademark and logo of Abdo Kids.

Printed in the United States of America, North Mankato, Minnesota.

102021

012022

THIS BOOK CONTAINS
RECYCLED MATERIALS

Photo Credits: Shutterstock

Production Contributors: Teddy Borth, Jennie Forsberg, Grace Hansen

Design Contributors: Candice Keimig, Pakou Moua

Library of Congress Control Number: 2021940305

Publisher's Cataloging-in-Publication Data

Names: King, Joe, author.

Title: Gross jokes / by Joe King

Description: Minneapolis, Minnesota : Abdo Kids, 2022 | Series: Abdo kids jokes | Includes online resource.

Identifiers: ISBN 9781098209179 (lib. bdg.) | ISBN 9781644946312 (pbk.) | ISBN 9781098209872 (ebook)
    | ISBN 9781098260231 (Read-to-Me ebook)

Subjects: LCSH: Jokes--Juvenile literature. | Wit and humor--Juvenile literature. | Aversion--Juvenile
    literature.

Classification: DDC 818.602--dc23

Table of Contents

Gross Jokes

What launches out of your
nose at thousands of miles
per hour?

A snot rocket!

What kind of spread goes
on a bagel with allergies?

Cream sneeze!

4

How do you get a tissue to dance?

You put a little boogie in it!

5

What's the difference between
roast beef and pea soup?

Anyone can roast beef!
But can anyone pea soup?

Why did Tigger stick his
head in the toilet?

He was looking for Pooh!

Why can't you hear a pterodactyl go to the bathroom?
Because the P is silent.
PTRULY PFUNNY!
SHHHH...
7

Knock Knock!

    Who's there?

I eat mop.

    I eat mop who?

You eat your poo?! Gross!

What's brown and sounds

like a bell?

DUNG!

8

Why did the toilet paper roll down the hill?
To get to the bottom!
TP!
WEEE!
9

How do you make a regular bath into a bubble bath?

Eat beans for dinner.

What do you call a dinosaur fart?

A blast from the past!

Why are ninja farts so dangerous?
They're silent but deadly.
UH OH...
RUN AWAY!
11

Why should you never fart on an elevator?

Because it's wrong on so many levels.

Why did the man stop telling fart jokes?

Everyone told him they stink.

What did the left eye say to the right eye?

Between us, something smells!

13

Why do vampires seem
sick all the time?

They're always coffin!

Why did Dracula go
to jail?

He robbed a blood bank!

14

Why didn't the skeleton cross the road?
He didn't have the guts!
JUST!
BONES!

Why was 6 so mad at 7?

Because 7, 8, 9!

Why did the cookie have
to go to the doctor?

It was feeling crummy.

What happened to the kid who drank eight sodas?

He burped 7-Up!

17

Why does everyone want to hang out with the mushroom?

*He's a **fungi**!*

What's brown and sticky?

A stick.

18

What's worse than finding a worm in your apple?

Finding half a worm.

Why was the computer so
embarrassed?

*Because he had software and
hardware, but no underwear!*

What does a storm cloud
wear under his pants?

Thunderwear!

Why do pirates wear underwear?

*To hide their **booty!***

21

Joke-Telling Tips!

- Know your audience

- Timing is everything

- Confidence is key

- Go out on a high note!

Glossary

booty

slang for pirate treasure.

fungi

living things that look like plants but eat other living matter.

pun

a joke using a word that sounds like a different word or has another meaning. Examples from this book are "cream sneeze" (cream cheese) and "coffin" (coughing).

Index

Abdo Kids ONLINE

FREE! ONLINE MULTIMEDIA RESOURCES

Visit **abdokids.com** to access crafts, games, videos, and more!

Use Abdo Kids code

AGK9179

or scan this QR code!